Knowing My GOD

Jesus Inspires Me

An enriching activity and coloring book

By Missi Jay

Graham Blanchard

Children's books for growing up in God

www.grahamblanchard.com

Meet the Soul Mates!

These Soul Mates are friends for life
who follow and love Jesus.
Will you be a Soul Mate, too?
Come along and create with them!

Know the heart
LEARN
and mind of Jesus

INSPIRE

say it like this:
N·SP·eye·RRR

Inspire means to give others
feelings that move them to
do or create something,
usually for the greater good.

How does Jesus inspire you?

Circle and color all the ways Jesus inspires you:

Now draw your own here!

Hello, my name is:

I am named after Silas, who traveled with the apostle Paul,

Timothy, and others to spread the word about Jesus.

They had tough times! But Silas was a reliable friend.

My favorite color is: Purple

My favorite things are: Space, grapes, fireflies, and penguins

The best things about me: I'm trustworthy, good at keeping my promises,

and I work really hard—especially on my soccer team.

"Come to me,"
Jesus said.

—Matthew 11:28 (NIV)

Find your way home

Owls rest in the day and work at night. Owls have special eyes that help them find their way through the dark. When you trust in Jesus, you use your special sense called *faith* to help you find your way.

Start

Home

"I have come into the world
as a light," Jesus said.

—John 12:46 (NIV)

"I know my sheep and my sheep know me," Jesus said.

—John 10:14 (NIV)

This for may be the MOMENT which you have been CREATED

-ESTHER 4:14

Hello, my name is:

I am named after Miriam, the brave sister of Moses and Aaron. As a girl, Miriam saved baby Moses. Later, she joined her brothers in leading their people to freedom.

My favorite color is: RED

My favorite things are: Ladybugs, birds, strawberries, and cherries

The best things about me: I'm friendly, bold, and my parents tell me I'm a helpful big sister!

"My command is this: Love each other as I have loved you," Jesus said.

—John 15:12 (NIV)

She is clothed with STRENGTH and DIGNITY AND SHE LAUGHS without fear of THE FUTURE

-PROVERBS 31:25 (NLT)

Secret message

The Soul Mates have left you a message. Use the alphabet decoder to fill in each blank with the letter that represents the picture under it. Do you know the answer to the question? What would the code be for it?

What's inside?

How do you get closer to God, who is unseen?
He comes to live with you in spirit, in your heart.

WORDS & SPIRIT of CHRIST

FAITH & UNITY WITH GOD

SPIRIT

ABOVE ALL ELSE, GUARD your HEART, FOR EVERYTHING YOU DO FLOWS from it. –PROVERBS 4:23 (NIV)

Be STRONG AND COURAGEOUS

DO NOT Be AFRAID
DO NOT Be DISCOURAGED
FOR THE LORD
YOUR GOD
WILL Be WITH YOU
WHEREVER YOU GO.
— JOSHUA 1:9 (NIV)

This is how I talk with God

To pray means to talk with God and stay close to him. Prayer grows our love for God and others. What do you want to talk with God about today?

Hello, my name is:

SETH

I am named after Seth, the third son of Adam and Eve. Seth and his family worshipped God. Did you know Jesus was born from the family line of Seth?

My favorite color is: Yellow (hello!)

My favorite things are: Sunshine, school, pineapples, balloons, and ducks

The best things about me: I'm cheerful, patient (sometimes), smart, and I ALMOST ALWAYS remember to say "Thank You!"

God's promise

When you read your Bible, you find out that God makes many promises.
He keeps them all! God says the rainbow is a sign for you.

See Genesis 9:8-17

Dot-to-dot

Start with 1 and connect the dots in counting order to reveal the baby's mother.
Then, decorate your own original picture by choosing different colors to fill them in.

We Love because He first Loved us.

-1 John 4:19 (NIV)

Barnacle or Jellyfish?

The barnacles clinging to the bottom of this boat will go wherever the boat goes.
The jellyfish and seahorse just drift along wherever the waves take them.
When you trust in Jesus, you are like a barnacle—choosing to cling to him!

Hello, my name is:

Priscilla

I am named after Priscilla, who loved to teach about Jesus in her home alongside her faithful husband, Aquila. They are always mentioned together in the Bible, and Paul honored them.

My favorite color is: Green!

My favorite things are: Apples, outdoors, trees, flowers, frogs, and worms

The best things about me: Smart, Kind to others, and I always try to make my friends laugh!

Spot the differences

Can you find 12 differences (that's a dozen!) in the two scenes below?
Try using different colors to make each scene different, too.

WITH GOD

ALL THINGS ARE POSSIBLE

—MATTHEW 19:26

Hello, what is YOUR name?

THIS IS YOU!

YOU'RE AMAZING

What is your favorite color? _____

What are your favorite things? _____

What are the best things about you? _____

OUR PRAYER FOR: YOU!

MAY the LORD BLESS YOU AND KEEP YOU;
MAY the LORD MAKE HIS FACE SHINE UPON YOU AND BE GRACIOUS TO YOU;
MAY the LORD TURN HIS FACE TOWARD YOU AND GIVE YOU PEACE.

AMEN!
That means "SO BE IT!"

—Numbers 6:24-27

Take some Time to DOODLE AWHILE

DRAW some Things that make you smile! 🙂

Answers

Look up into the heavens.
Who created all the stars?
— Isaiah 40:26

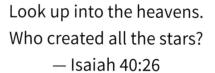

Graham
Blanchard

Children's books for growing up in God

Graham Blanchard Inc. | P.O. Box 300235, Austin, Texas, 78703 | **www.grahamblanchard.com**

ISBN: 978-0-9897949-7-8

By Missi Jay
Editorial: Callie Grant, Audra Haney, and Charissa Kolar

Printed in the United States of America